SOUTH
CAROLINA

Hello U★S★A★

SOUTH CAROLINA

Charles Fredeen

Lerner Publications Company

Cover photograph courtesy of © Jay Browne, S. C. Forestry Commission.

The glossary that begins on page 68 gives definitions of words shown in **bold type** in the text.

LIBRARY OF CONGRESS
CATALOGING-IN-PUBLICATION DATA
Fredeen, Charles.
    South Carolina / Charles Fredeen.
       p.   cm. — (Hello USA)
    Includes index.
    Summary: Introduces the geography, history, people, industries, and other highlights of South Carolina.
    ISBN 0-8225-2712-X (lib. bdg.)
    1. South Carolina—Juvenile literature.
[1. South Carolina.] I. Title. II. Series.
F269.3.F74 1991
975.2—dc20   90-13532

Manufactured in the United States of America
3 4 5 6 7 - JR - 00 99 98 97 96

 This book is printed on acid-free, recyclable paper.

CONTENTS

Did You Know . . . ?

☐ The longest sand sculpture in the world was built in 1990 on Myrtle Beach, South Carolina. Created by 1,613 people, the sculpture stretched more than 10 miles (16 kilometers)!

☐ In 1890 a South Carolinian started the first tea farm to earn money in the United States.

☐ On a hike in South Carolina, you may discover one of the state's 43 kinds of snakes slithering across the trail. Most of these snakes are harmless, but some—including the rattlesnake, copperhead, and coral snake—have poisonous bites.

☐ The bones of the largest seabird ever known were found near Charleston, South Carolina, in 1984. The bird, which lived about 30 million years ago, is called a pseudodontorn, or bony-toothed bird. It probably weighed 100 pounds (45 kilograms) and could spread its wings 18 feet (5.5 meters) wide.

☐ On Christmas Day 1830, the first working steam locomotive built in the United States chugged out of Charleston with 141 passengers. With that trip, the "Best Friend of Charleston" began the first regular railroad passenger service in the country.

A Trip Around the State

Hurricane Hugo, one of the worst hurricanes ever to hit South Carolina, flattened parts of this southern state in 1989. Powerful winds blew down one-third of South Carolina's trees, and 70,000 people lost their homes. For weeks, fallen trees and other wreckage blocked 18,000 miles (28,962 km) of roads. South Carolina's two neighboring states, Georgia and North Carolina, also suffered damage.

Most of the destroyed buildings and fallen trees were on the Coastal Plain, one of South Carolina's three land regions. South Carolinians call the Coastal Plain the Low Country because it is so close to sea level. The Piedmont and the Blue Ridge Mountains, the state's two other regions, together are called the Up Country because they rise higher than the Coastal Plain.

9

Bald cypress trees thrive in warm swampy areas.

The Coastal Plain covers the southeastern half of South Carolina. Thousands of years ago, the Atlantic Ocean swelled over most of the low-lying plain. When the ocean pulled back to its present shoreline, it left the sandy soil that now blankets the Coastal Plain.

The low, flat part of the Coastal Plain stretches inland past the **swamps,** or wetlands, that soak much of the Low Country. To the northwest, the plain rises into rolling hills of sand that are covered with pine forests.

10

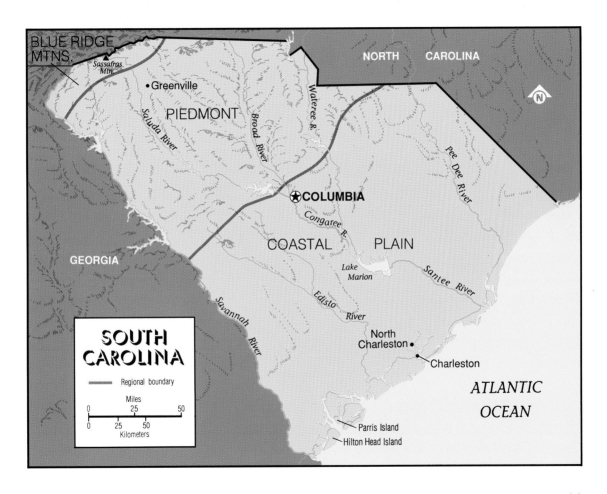

BLUE RIDGE MTNS.

Sassafras Mtn

• Greenville

PIEDMONT

Saluda River

Broad River

Wateree R.

NORTH CAROLINA

N

Pee Dee River

★COLUMBIA

Congaree R.

COASTAL PLAIN

GEORGIA

Lake Marion

Santee River

Edisto River

Savannah River

North Charleston •

Charleston

ATLANTIC OCEAN

Parris Island

Hilton Head Island

SOUTH CAROLINA

Regional boundary

Miles
0   25   50

0   25   50
Kilometers

11

These sand hills divide the Coastal Plain from the Piedmont, a higher, rockier region that covers most of northwestern South Carolina. The Piedmont's forested hills slope down toward the Coastal Plain. As the rivers of the rocky Up Country tumble down onto the sandy Low Country, they form a series of waterfalls called the Fall Line.

The Blue Ridge Mountains pass through a tiny sliver of land along South Carolina's northwestern border. Pine-covered peaks stand out among the rolling hills and valleys of the Blue Ridge. Sassafras Mountain, the state's highest point, overlooks this region.

Several rivers run across South Carolina. The Santee River and its major branches—the Wateree and the Congaree—divide the state in half. In eastern South Carolina, the Pee Dee River enters the state near the Fall Line. The Savannah River marks the border between South Carolina and Georgia. Other rivers include the Edisto, the Broad, and the Saluda.

12

A bluish mist settles over the rolling Blue Ridge Mountain region.

13

Waterfalls spill over the rocky areas along South Carolina's Fall Line.

Many dams have been built on the state's rivers. The dams collect water for **hydropower,** or water power. When released, the water turns wheels that generate electricity for use in homes and businesses. Water held back by the dams also creates most of South Carolina's lakes, including Lake Marion, the biggest.

Hot, sticky summers and mild winters are typical of South Carolina's climate. July temperatures hover around 90° F (32° C), but the mountains are usually cooler. In winter, the Blue Ridge Mountains block cold air from the northwest, keeping temperatures in the state well above freezing.

Rainfall is plentiful in most parts of South Carolina, with an average of 45 inches (114 centimeters) measured each year. Snow rarely falls except in the mountains, which get more moisture overall than the rest of the state. Tornadoes and hurricanes sometimes threaten South Carolina's people, cities, and land.

Fierce hurricanes can strike the coast of South Carolina, causing damage to both the land and buildings.

  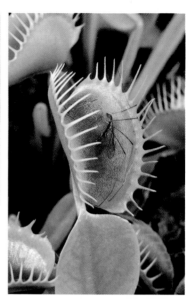

Pitcher plant *(left)*
Passionflower *(center)*
Venus's-flytrap *(right)*

Although hurricanes occasionally uproot trees in South Carolina, forests still cover much of the state. Pines, tulip trees, cottonwoods, and magnolias grow throughout South Carolina. Webs of Spanish moss, a flowering plant with no roots, hang from cypress and live oak trees.

Azaleas and laurels brighten the Carolina countryside in the spring. And insects should be wary here.

South Carolina is one of only two states where Venus's-flytrap, a bug-eating plant, grows wild. (It also grows in North Carolina.)

The swamps of the Coastal Plain shelter many alligators and a few black bears. The region also hosts flocks of ducks and geese during the winter. Clams, crabs, and shrimp live just off the Carolina coast in the Atlantic Ocean. Plenty of white-tailed deer bound through the forests of the Piedmont and the Blue Ridge Mountains, sharing the woods with opossums, rabbits, raccoons, and wildcats.

An alligator slithers into one of South Carolina's swamps.

King Charles I

South Carolina's Story

South Carolina was named for King Charles I of Great Britain. (*Carolina* comes from the Latin word for "Charles.") But the state's story begins long before the king's reign.

Thousands of years ago, more than 25 different American Indian groups lived in the hills and lowlands of what is now South Carolina. Most of the tribes lived in villages. For food, the Indians grew crops, fished, and hunted wild game.

For centuries, Indians in South Carolina farmed and hunted just outside their villages.

Deer often fell to Cherokee bows and arrows. To get closer to the deer, hunters sometimes covered themselves with deerskins that still had the head and antlers attached.

By the 1500s, one of the largest Indian nations was the Catawba, a powerful tribe that built its villages near the Wateree River. The Catawba grew corn, squash, beans, and gourds. When the Indians needed meat, they hunted deer or fished the rivers.

The Cherokee, another large, powerful tribe, lived in South Carolina's Up Country. Like the Catawba, the Cherokee built villages along rivers and streams. The Cherokee grew a lot of maize, or corn. They cooked maize by roasting or boiling it—just like we cook corn. The Cherokee also gathered crab apples, cherries, chestnuts, and other wild plant foods.

Some of these Indians may have met Europeans for the first time in 1521, when a group of Spaniards explored the Carolina coast. Forty years later, the French tried to settle in the same area. Plagued by hunger and disease, both European groups returned to their homelands shortly after arriving.

A statue in Fort Mill, South Carolina, honors a Catawba hunter.

King Charles II

Great Britain was the next European country to take an interest in the Carolina coast. In the early 1600s, Great Britain claimed territory in North America that included what is now South Carolina, North Carolina, and Georgia. Fifty years later, in 1663, King Charles II of Britain gave this territory, called Carolina, to eight wealthy British men. These men paid people from Great Britain to move to Carolina and start a **colony,** or settlement.

In Britain, the settlers loaded up their ships with food and other necessities. Their cargo included three

Africans, who were among the earliest black slaves in the South. The settlers arrived in 1670 and built South Carolina's first permanent colony at Albemarle Point, near where Charleston is now.

The British colonists soon angered several of South Carolina's Indian tribes. Many white traders, who bought thousands of deerskins from the Indians each year, treated the Native Americans poorly. Traders kidnapped hundreds of Indian women and children and forced them to become slaves. The traders then killed Indian men who tried to save their families.

Indians greet the British newcomers who arrived at Albemarle Point in 1670.

The Yamasee War of 1715 marked the disappearance of the Yamasee Indians. Those who survived the war settled with other tribes in Florida and soon lost their Yamasee customs.

When the colonists built a new town on land that belonged to the Yamasee Indians, the Yamasee attacked white settlements, killing 90 settlers and traders. Fifteen other tribes, including the powerful Catawba, fought with the Yamasee in the war that followed. It ended less than two years later, when an army of settlers drove the Yamasee south into Florida.

Many Indians died in the Yamasee War. But these losses soon seemed small compared to the number of Indians who died from diseases brought by the Europeans. Eventually, only small groups of Indians were left in the region.

Stede Bonnet

Pirates were a constant threat to ships sailing in and out of the Charleston Harbor in the early 1700s. In 1718 South Carolinians finally captured one of the most wicked villains—Stede Bonnet.

Bonnet and his crew had sailed into a hiding place along the Carolina coast one night. The governor of South Carolina learned that Bonnet lurked outside the colony and sent Colonel William Rhett to capture the outlaw.

Rhett soon found the pirates. As Bonnet tried to escape, Rhett sailed after him until both ships suddenly ground to a halt. Bonnet and Rhett were stuck on a sandbar.

The men waited five hours for the ocean tide to rise. The force of the tide soon freed Rhett's ship. The pirates, still stuck, surrendered in fright.

Rhett brought the captives back to Charleston. Twenty-nine members of Bonnet's crew were hanged. Bonnet escaped but was recaptured and hanged one month after the rest of his gang.

In the early 1700s, Great Britain carved two new colonies from Carolina. The northern portion became North Carolina, and Georgia was set up in the south, leaving South Carolina in between. South Carolina was now one of 13 British colonies in North America. To help increase the colony's population, South Carolina welcomed immigrants from Germany, Ireland, and other European countries.

These newcomers were unlike the earlier settlers. The first colo-

By 1740 Charleston was one of the busiest cities in the North American colonies. More than 200 ships a year carried goods into the Charleston Harbor.

Before the 1800s, rice was South Carolina's most important crop.

nists, who lived in the Low Country, had come mostly from Britain and had similar customs. They earned their money by growing crops on plantations, or large farms, and they used slaves to work the plantations.

The later immigrants, who settled in the state's Up Country, came from many countries, each with different customs. Most of these new settlers owned small farms, so they didn't use slaves. The differences between the Up Country and the Low Country made the two regions seem like separate countries.

During the Revolution, colonial soldiers attacked and defeated British forces at the Battle of Kings Mountain in South Carolina.

As more settlers came to South Carolina, the British king forced them to pay new taxes and to follow new laws. Although South Carolinians disagreed on many things, most of them agreed that the king had no right to make them pay these taxes. In 1775 South Carolina joined the 12 other colonies in a fight for their independence from Britain. This fight became known as the American Revolution.

During the Revolution, which lasted eight years, 137 battles were fought in South Carolina—more than in any other colony. In 1781 colonial soldiers forced the British army out of South Carolina. By 1783 Britain had lost the war, and the colonists formed their own country—the United States of America. South Carolina joined the Union in 1788, becoming the new country's eighth state.

General Francis Marion (center) and his colonial soldiers camped in South Carolina's wet, insect-filled swamps and lived on sweet potatoes and corn during the Revolution.

After the war, cotton became South Carolina's most important crop when an inventor named Eli Whitney built the cotton gin. This machine pulled cotton fibers—used to make cloth—from cotton seeds 50 times faster than people could. As cotton plantations grew, South Carolina's planters depended more heavily on slave labor to pick cotton from the fields.

Like many other Southern states, South Carolina had been getting slaves from Africa to work on rice and indigo (a source of blue dye) plantations. With the rise of the cotton industry, planters bought even more slaves. Soon more slaves than free people lived in the state. White planters began to worry that slaves might organize an uprising. If they did, the outnumbered planters could lose all their power and property.

South Carolinians also worried that the U.S. government was paying more attention to the concerns of Northerners than to those of Southerners. Unlike the South, where crops were the greatest money-makers, the North earned much of its money from manufactured goods. The U.S. government wanted to make sure that Americans bought the products made by Northern factories.

South Carolina shipped tons of cotton to Britain each year after 1800. The state depended on this trade to get almost all of the manufactured goods it needed.

To do this, the government raised the **tariffs**, or fees, it charged on goods bought from other countries. The tariff made foreign products more expensive to buy. Because South Carolina's planters depended on trade with Britain, they began to lose money when they traded their cotton for British goods.

For the next several decades, the North and South had many clashes, especially about slavery. Many Northerners thought slavery was cruel and should be outlawed. Many Southerners disagreed. Abraham Lincoln, a Northerner, was elected president of the United States in 1860. The people of the

South Carolinian John C. Calhoun *(pointing)* argued that his state could disobey U.S. tariff laws that hurt South Carolina's interests. He believed that a state's rights were more important than those of the country as a whole.

At slave auctions, slave traders set up a platform and sold men, women, and children to plantation owners.

South believed Lincoln would use his power to rid the South of slavery, which could lead Southerners into poverty.

To protect itself from financial ruin, South Carolina decided to **secede** (withdraw) from the United States. Ten other Southern states followed South Carolina. The eleven former states formed their own country—the Confederate States of America. Soon, the United States and the Confederate States were at war.

At the start of the Civil War, Confederate troops sent cannonballs sailing into Fort Sumter.

The first shots of the Civil War were fired on April 12, 1861, when Confederate troops fired at Fort Sumter, a Union fort in South Carolina's Charleston Harbor. Thirty-four hours later, the outnumbered Northern troops were defeated. Despite all the exploding shells, there was only one death in battle—a horse.

In 1865 Union troops invaded South Carolina and set Columbia, the capital city, ablaze *(below)*. When the soldiers left, the city lay in ruins *(left)*.

South Carolina's state flag, designed in 1776, represented the Confederacy during the Civil War. It became the state flag again when South Carolina rejoined the Union in 1868.

About 600,000 soldiers, however, would die during the next four years of the Civil War. More than 10,000 South Carolinians lost their lives in fierce and bloody battles before the South surrendered to the North in 1865.

The Civil War left much of South Carolina in ruins. Its capital city, Columbia, had been burned to the ground by Union troops. Other cities, homes, plantations, and crops had been destroyed throughout the state.

President Lincoln had freed the slaves, but most of them had no money, no home, and no job. They could not even afford to move to the North, where there were more jobs. Many black families became **sharecroppers,** farming another person's land and receiving a small share of the crops they grew as payment for their labor.

For the next 12 years, Union soldiers lived in South Carolina to oversee **Reconstruction,** or the rebuilding of the South. In 1868 a new state constitution gave black men the right to vote. The U.S. government then allowed South Carolina to rejoin the United States.

Wade Hampton (*lifting hat*)**,** South Carolina's first governor after Reconstruction, vowed to treat all South Carolinians fairly. To do this, he selected many black people for government jobs.

In the late 1800s, whole families, including children, worked 16-hour days in the textile mills of the Up Country.

South Carolina recovered slowly from the Civil War. Some planters started growing cotton again, but many farmers couldn't afford to hire former slaves or to rebuild their farms. They turned instead to manufacturing. In the Up Country, mills were built to make textiles, or cloth. Workers earned only 72 cents a day, but people welcomed any job they could find.

The state's growing textile industry did not help black people. Most mills refused to give jobs to African Americans. In the late 1800s, lawmakers passed what became known as **Jim Crow laws**. These laws required people of different skin color to use separate schools, hospitals, drinking fountains, and telephone booths. Blacks couldn't use the same rest rooms as whites or go to the same hotels or restaurants.

Black people could not change these laws because white lawmakers had found ways to prevent African Americans from voting. Many of them left South Carolina and moved to northern cities, where they hoped they would have better opportunities. From the 1940s to the 1960s, African Americans throughout the country joined the **civil rights movement,** fighting to end the Jim Crow laws and to win equal voting rights.

During the same period, facto-

Signs like this one hung in South Carolinian towns until the civil rights movement ended Jim Crow laws.

ries spread throughout South Carolina and manufacturing became more important than agriculture. As the state began to make more money from manufacturing, it also began to pay attention to the issues of the civil rights movement.

39

Native Americans enter what is now South Carolina

Spaniards reach the Carolina coast

First settlement is built at Albemarle Point

Settlers and Indians fight the Yamasee War

South Carolina becomes the eighth state to join the Union

Since 1970 factories and offices in South Carolina have been opening their doors to black workers. Progress has been made toward the goal of equal rights. Now white students and African American students can sit side by side in South Carolina's classrooms. In 1983, I. DeQuincey Newman became the first black state senator since Reconstruction. In politics, at their jobs, and in schools, South Carolinians are trying to make their state a better place to live.

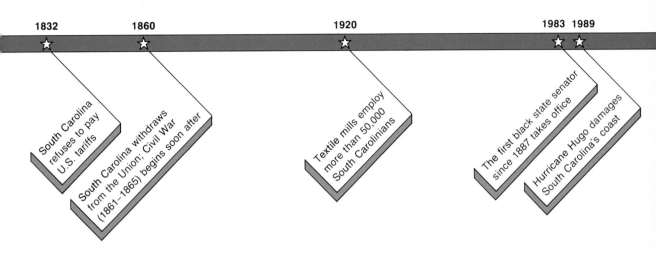

1832 South Carolina refuses to pay U.S. tariffs

1860 South Carolina withdraws from the Union; Civil War (1861–1865) begins soon after

1920 Textile mills employ more than 50,000 South Carolinians

1983 The first black state senator since 1887 takes office

1989 Hurricane Hugo damages South Carolina's coast

41

Living and Working in South Carolina

The differences between black people and white people and between the Up Country and the Low Country are no longer as great as they once were. Whether in cotton fields, textile mills, or government offices, South Carolina's 3.5 million people are working together.

More than half of South Carolina's population lives in cities. Columbia, the state's capital and largest city, sprawls along the border between the Low Country and the Up Country. Historic Charleston, full of old gardens and mansions, is the second largest city. North Charleston and Greenville are the only other cities that have more than 50,000 people.

Most of the people who live in South Carolina were born in South Carolina. Many of them come from families that have lived in the area since colonial days. Two out of three South Carolinians have European ancestors.

African Americans make up slightly less than one-third of the population. Along the southeastern coast, some of them speak their own language, called **Gullah**—a mixture of African languages, colonial English, and the American En-

glish spoken today. Many of the state's 6,000 American Indians are Catawba. Small numbers of Hispanics and Asians make up the rest of the state's population.

History surrounds South Carolinians. Revolutionary battles were fought at a number of sites, including Cowpens and Kings Mountain. At Fort Sumter, visitors can imagine hearing the sound of the first shots of the Civil War. Old buildings, houses, and plantations are scattered throughout the state.

Crafts and traditions from many cultures have been passed down from parent to child through generations of South Carolinians.

The Fighting Gamecocks run for a touchdown.

The Charleston Museum, one of the oldest museums in the United States, displays colonial tools and homes. The South Carolina State Museum in Columbia traces South Carolina's history. Other museums in the state exhibit everything from gospel music to military missiles.

One of the most famous museums is the Stock Car Hall of Fame in Darlington. Thousands of people visit this museum when they come to the Transouth 500 Stock Car Race each April. Other sports fans in South Carolina cheer on the Clemson Tigers or the University of South Carolina's Fighting Gamecocks, two college football teams.

South Carolina's beaches and mountains also make the state a fun place to be. People enjoy swimming, boating, and tennis, especially at seaside resorts such as Hilton Head. This island off the Atlantic coast has everything from nature walks to championship golf courses. On the other side of the state, hiking in the Blue Ridge Mountains is a popular activity.

46

At a beach on Hilton Head Island, a family sculpts a sandcastle.

Tourism is a steady source of money and jobs for the state. People who work in jobs that serve tourists—in restaurants or hotels, for example—have service jobs. South Carolina also has many other types of service jobs. Some service workers sell or trade food, fabric, or clothing. Columbia and Charleston are important trading centers.

Government jobs, including those in the military, are also service jobs. Parris Island, located at the

Soldiers at Fort Jackson in Columbia take a break from their tough training.

A truck dumps its load of wood chips into a factory yard.

workers earn almost two-thirds of the state's money.

After services, manufacturing brings the most money to South Carolina. One out of three people in the Up Country works in a factory, most likely a textile mill. Millworkers make $2 billion worth of cotton, silk, wool, and other fabrics each year. South Carolina makes more cloth than any other state except North Carolina. Other factory workers make fertilizers, chemicals, and paper.

southern end of the state's coast, has the country's largest training base for the U.S. Marines. Charleston has both a naval and an airforce base. South Carolina's service

Peaches *(left)*
Soybeans *(below)*

Agriculture is no longer a big business in South Carolina. It earns only 1 percent of the state's money and employs only 3 percent of the state's workers, mostly in the Low Country. Cotton is still grown, but tobacco is the state's largest crop. South Carolina is a leading producer of peaches. Soybeans and corn are also major crops. Most livestock farmers raise cows or chickens.

Power shovels scoop kaolin out of a surface mine.

The earth beneath South Carolina's plains and mountains provides jobs, too. Miners cut limestone from the Low Country and carve slabs of granite from the Up Country. Both limestone and granite are used in roads and buildings. Kaolin, a chalky white clay, and marl, a crumbly substance used in cement and fertilizer, are some of the state's other minerals.

Fishing boats nestle in a harbor.

Shrimp may be small compared to other fish, but they make up a big share of South Carolina's seafood industry. Shrimp are the most valuable part of the state's fishing catch, which includes crabs, oysters, and clams caught along the Carolina coast.

South Carolina is not the same as it was 200 years ago. What was once an Indian village or a cotton plantation may now be the site of a mill or factory. But the beauty of the state remains. From the mountain waterfalls of the Up Country to the wide, white beaches of the Low Country, South Carolina remains a jewel of the South.

Protecting the Environment

On summer nights, huge sea turtles crawl out of the Atlantic Ocean onto South Carolina's beaches. The turtles use their flippers to dig nests in the sand, where they lay 35 to 180 eggs. Minutes later, the turtles cover their eggs with sand and crawl back to the sea.

The turtles are called logger-heads. The biggest loggerheads can weigh as much as 400 pounds (181 kg), but their eggs are smaller than Ping-Pong balls. Eight weeks after the eggs are laid, tiny baby turtles called hatchlings dig them-selves out of their buried nests.

A loggerhead turtle lays her eggs in a sandy nest.

After wiggling from its shell and digging out of its nest, a hatchling is ready to crawl to the ocean.

The first few days of a loggerhead's life are filled with danger. Sea gulls, raccoons, dogs, hogs, and ghost crabs like to eat the hatchlings. Even if they don't get eaten, the hatchlings will dry up and die unless they find water. To survive, they must crawl quickly from their nests to the protection of the ocean.

For centuries, the young turtles have left their nests at night (when most birds do not hunt) and have easily found the water. But in recent years, fewer loggerhead hatchlings have survived the crawl to the ocean. The reason—people.

More and more people have homes close to South Carolina's beaches. More and more tourists visit the seashore each year. This means more cars and other vehicles drive across the sand and more lights shine on the beach.

At night, away from artificial lights, water appears brighter than land because water reflects the natural light from the sky. Scientists believe that natural light guides loggerhead hatchlings to the water.

But near resorts and towns, some turtles get confused by all the streetlights and spotlights. They crawl toward these lights

Hatchlings head for the sea.

and end up on roads or highways, where they are often crushed by oncoming traffic. Others aren't sure which way to go. They wander on the beach until they are eaten or until they dry up and die.

This truck is helping rebuild a beach that has lost much of its sand. But trucks can hurt loggerhead hatchlings by packing down the sand with their wide wheels.

When people drive cars on the beach, they may unknowingly kill turtles even before they hatch. Cars are heavy. They pack down the sand, making it hard. Oxygen, which the turtle eggs need to develop, cannot always pass through the hardened sand. Eggs that don't get enough oxygen will not hatch. Even if the eggs do hatch, not all hatchlings can dig through the hardened sand, and they die in their nests.

In packed sand, female turtles may not be able to dig a nest deep enough to protect their eggs. Hard sand may even keep females from digging nests at all. The turtles may return to the ocean without laying any eggs.

Scientists call problems like the ones facing loggerheads "loss of habitat." Because the turtles are losing their habitat, fewer and fewer loggerheads live along the coast of South Carolina. The population of loggerheads has dropped so much that South Carolina has added the animal to the state's list of endangered and threatened species. This means that the turtle is in danger of becoming extinct.

Volunteers check South Carolina's loggerhead population by counting the empty turtle eggshells on the beach.

Scientists who have studied loggerhead turtles have ideas about how to help more hatchlings survive the crawl to the ocean. Trapping the animals that eat the hatchlings can save many young turtles. Putting wire screens around the nests to prevent predators from eating the eggs can also help.

Some scientists think the problems caused by packed sand and streetlights can be solved by carefully moving turtle nests away from the beaches that people use. Streetlights can be shaded by plants, fences, or other barriers to keep artificial light from reaching the beach.

South Carolinians want to protect the loggerhead from extinction. Scientists have been able to help other threatened animals, such as the bald eagle. Many South Carolinians hope scientists can save the loggerhead, too.

South Carolina's Famous People

ACTIVISTS

Mary McLeod Bethune (1875–1955), an educator, grew up in Mayesville, South Carolina. She moved to Florida and started a school for black girls, which later became Bethune-Cookman College. She was president of the college for 20 years.

Angelina Emily Grimke (1805–1879) and **Sarah Moore Grimke** (1792–1873), sisters, were born in Charleston. The Grimke sisters worked to end slavery and to gain rights for women. They wrote pamphlets and were among the first women in the country to give public speeches.

Jesse Jackson (born 1941), from Greenville, South Carolina, is a Baptist minister and a civil rights leader. Jackson ran for U.S. president in 1984 and 1988, and in 1990 he was elected as acting Senator for Washington, D.C.

◀ MARY McLEOD BETHUNE

▲ ANGELINA and SARAH GRIMKE ▲

◀ JESSE JACKSON

JOSEPH FRAZIER ▶

ATHLETES

Joseph Frazier (born 1944) is known as Smokin' Joe in the boxing world. Born in Beaufort, South Carolina, Frazier won an Olympic gold medal in 1964 and was the professional heavyweight champion from 1970 to 1973.

Althea Gibson (born 1927), born in Silver, South Carolina, won the women's singles title at both Wimbledon and the U.S. National Tennis Championships in 1957 and 1958. She was the first black woman to win either of these tournaments.

◀ WADE HAMPTON

Wade Hampton (1818–1902), born in Charleston, led Confederate soldiers in the Civil War. When he became governor of South Carolina in 1876, Hampton worked to make the state's government fair. He appointed black people to state offices and supported voting rights for black men.

Francis Marion (1732?–1795), nicknamed the "Swamp Fox," was a commander during the American Revolution. Born and raised near Winyah, South Carolina, he used his knowledge of the state's marshes to fight the British forces.

Robert Smalls (1839–1915) was born a slave in Beaufort, South Carolina. During the Civil War, the Confederacy forced Smalls to pilot a ship. One night, he took command of the ship, sailed it into Union hands, and became a Union hero. After the war, Smalls represented South Carolina in both the state and the U.S. legislatures.

▲ FRANCIS MARION

◀ ROBERT SMALLS

◀ ARTHUR FREED

DIZZY
GILLESPIE ▶

MUSICIANS & SONGWRITERS

Arthur Freed (1894–1973), born in Charleston, wrote "Singin' in the Rain" and many other hit songs. He also produced 40 movie musicals, including *The Wizard of Oz* and *Gigi.*

John Birks ("Dizzy") Gillespie (1917–1993) was a trumpet player, composer, and bandleader. In the 1940s, he helped to create a lively, fast-paced style of jazz called bebop. Gillespie was born in Cheraw, South Carolina.

▲ ERNEST HOLLINGS

John Caldwell Calhoun (1782–1850) served the U.S. government for forty years—four of them as vice president. He was born in Abbeville District, South Carolina, and is remembered for his strong support of slavery and of states' rights.

Ernest Frederick Hollings (born 1922) is from Charleston. A U.S. senator since 1966, Hollings has pushed for laws to protect wildlife and the environment. He served as South Carolina's governor from 1959 to 1963.

ANDREW ▶
JACKSON

▲ JOSEPH
RAINEY

Andrew Jackson (1767–1845), born in Waxhaw, South Carolina, fought in the revolutionary war when he was 13. He served as the seventh president of the United States from 1827 to 1837.

Joseph Hayne Rainey (1832–1887), a former slave and barber by occupation, was the first black man to serve in the U.S. House of Representatives. Born in Georgetown, South Carolina, Rainey was a representative from 1870 to 1879.

Benjamin Ryan Tillman (1847–1918), born in Edgefield County, was South Carolina's first governor from the Up Country. Nicknamed Pitchfork Ben, Tillman was disliked by many people for his angry speeches and his attacks on the powerful politicians of the Low Country. But he was the first governor to give the people of the Up Country a share of South Carolina's money and power.

◄ BENJAMIN TILLMAN

Ernest E. Just (1883–1941) was born in Charleston. In 1915 Just, a biologist who studied cell life, received the first Spingarn Medal, an award for excellence given yearly to a black person.

Ronald McNair (1950–1986) grew up in Lake City, South Carolina. An astronaut, he was the second black man to travel in space. McNair was killed when the space shuttle *Challenger* exploded on January 28, 1986.

Charles Hard Townes (born 1915) grew up outside Greenville, South Carolina. Townes and another American scientist introduced the ideas that led to the invention of the laser. This powerful light beam can be used in many ways, such as cutting steel and reading bar codes at the grocery store. Townes won the 1964 Nobel Prize in physics for his work.

▲ RONALD McNAIR
(top left)

CHARLES TOWNES ▶

◀ MAY CRAIG

DuBOSE
▼ HEYWARD

WRITERS

May Craig (1889–1975), born in Coosaw, South Carolina, was a journalist at a time when the field was dominated by men. Her newspaper articles and radio broadcasts focused on laws that affected women. During World War II, Craig reported from the front lines of battle in France and Germany.

DuBose Heyward (1885–1940), born in Charleston, wrote poetry and novels about South Carolina's black people. His novel *Porgy* was made into an opera. Heyward also wrote *Mamba's Daughter* and *Jasbo Brown and Selected Poems*.

Facts-at-a-Glance

Nickname: Palmetto State
Song: "Carolina"
Mottoes: *Animis Opibusque Parati (Prepared in Mind and Resources)* and *Dum Spiro, Spero* (While I Breathe, I Hope)
Flower: Carolina jessamine
Tree: palmetto
Bird: Carolina wren

Population: 3,486,703*
Rank in population, nationwide: 25th
Area: 31,113 sq mi (80,583 sq km)
Rank in area, nationwide: 40th
Date and ranking of statehood:
  May 23, 1788, the 8th state
Capital: Columbia
Major cities (and populations*):
  Columbia (98,052), Charleston (80,414), North Charleston (70,218), Greenville (58,282), Spartanburg (43,467)
U.S. senators: 2
U.S. representatives: 6
Electoral votes: 8

* 1990 census

Places to visit: Old Exchange and Provost Dungeon in Charleston, Cowpens National Battlefield near Gaffney, Cypress Gardens near Charleston, Stumphouse Mountain Tunnel near Walhalla, Whitewater Falls above Salem

Annual events: Governor's Annual Frog Jumping Contest in Springfield (Sat. before Easter), Catfish Festival in Ware Shoals (May), Gold Rush Days in McCormick (June), Water Festival in Beaufort (July), Chitlin Strut in Salley (Nov.)

66

Natural resources: soil, kaolin, marl, limestone, clay, gold, lumber, water, granite

Agricultural products: tobacco, soybeans, corn, peaches, eggs, chickens, beef cattle, hogs

Manufactured goods: textiles, clothing, chemicals, machinery, paper products, rubber and plastics products

ENDANGERED SPECIES
Mammals—eastern cougar
Birds—bald eagle, wood stork, red-cockaded wood-pecker, American swallow-tailed kite
Reptile—gopher tortoise
Fish—shortnose sturgeon
Plants—black-spored quillwort, persistent trillium, rough-leaved loosestrife, pondberry, Canby's dropwort

WHERE SOUTH CAROLINIANS WORK
Services—46 percent
(services includes jobs in trade; community, social, & personal services; finance, insurance, & real estate; transportation, communication, & utilities)
Manufacturing—28 percent
Government—18 percent
Construction—5 percent
Agriculture—3 percent

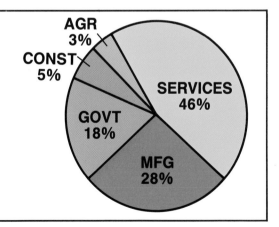

AGR 3%
CONST 5%
SERVICES 46%
GOVT 18%
MFG 28%

Albemarle (AL-buh-mahrl)

Catawba (kuh-TAW-buh)

Cherokee (CHEHR-uh-kee)

Confederate (kuhn-FEHD-uh-ruht)

Congaree (KAHNG-guh-ree)

Cowpens (KOW-PEHNZ)

Edisto (EHD-uh-stoh)

Gullah (GUHL-uh)

Piedmont (PEED-mahnt)

Saluda (suh-LOOD-uh)

Santee (SAN-TEE)

Sassafras (SAS-uh-fras)

Wateree (WAWT-uh-ree)

Yamasee (YAH-muh-see)

Glossary

civil rights movement   A movement to gain equal rights, or freedoms, for all citizens—regardless of race, religion, sex.

colony   A territory ruled by a country some distance away.

Gullah   The language that is spoken by a group of black people living along the coast and on the Sea Islands of the southeastern United States. Gullah is a combination of English and several African languages.

hydropower   The electricity produced by using waterpower. Also called hydro-electric power.

Jim Crow laws Measures that separate black people from white people in public places, such as schools, parks, theaters, and restaurants. Jim Crow laws were enforced in the U.S. South from 1877 to the 1950s.

Reconstruction The period from 1865 to 1877 during which the U.S. government brought the Southern states back into the Union after the Civil War. Before rejoining the Union, a Southern state had to pass a law allowing black men to vote. Places destroyed in the war were rebuilt and industries were developed.

secede To stop being a member of a political union or other group.

sharecropper A person who farms land that belongs to someone else. As payment for their labor, sharecroppers get a house, tools, and a share of the crops they grow.

swamp A wetland permanently soaked with water. Woody plants (trees and shrubs) are the main form of vegetation.

tariff A tax charged by a government on goods bought from or sold to other countries.

Index ━━━━━◣

Acknowledgments:

Maryland Cartographics, pp. 2, 11; © Jay Browne, S. C. Forestry Commission, pp. 2–3, 10, 13, 14, 42–43, 49; Myrtle Beach Chamber of Commerce, p. 6; Hilton Head Island Chamber of Commerce, p. 9 (left); South Carolina ETV, pp. 9 (top right), 15; Monica V. Brown, Photographic Artist, p. 9 (bottom right); Olde English District Commission, p. 16 (left); Jeff Greenberg, p. 16 (center); © Cabisco/Visuals Unlimited, p. 16 (right); © Tom J. Ulrich/Visuals Unlimited, p. 17; Library of Congress, pp. 18, 28, 29, 31, 34, 62 (center left, center right), 63 (top right, center), 64 (top left, center, bottom left, bottom right); From the Collection of the South Carolina State Museum, p. 19; By permission of the British Library, p. 20; Joanna Angle, pp. 21, 44–45; From the Collections of the South Carolina Historical Society, pp. 22, 25; South Caroliniana Library, University of South Carolina, pp. 23, 24, 26, 32, 33, 35, 36, 38, 65 (bottom right); Independent Picture Service, pp. 27, 62 (top, bottom right), 63 (top left, bottom left); The Bettmann Archive, p. 39; Tina Manley ©, pp. 41, 45 (right); Doyen Salsig, p. 44 (left); © Joseph L. Fontenot/Visuals Unlimited, pp. 46, 53; Sea Pines Plantation Company, Inc., Hilton Head Island, SC, p. 47; U.S. Army, Ft. Jackson, p. 48; South Carolina Department of Agriculture, p. 50; J. M. Huber Corporation, Langley, South Carolina, p. 51; South Carolina Department of Parks, Recreation, and Tourism, p. 55; © David S. Addison/Visuals Unlimited, p. 56; Lynn M. Stone, pp. 57, 59; Larry Cameron, Coastal Science and Engineering, Inc., p. 58; © Joel Arrington/Visuals Unlimited, p. 61; National Rainbow Coalition, p. 62 (bottom left); Schomburg Center for Research in Black Culture, NYPL, p. 63 (bottom right); National Archives, pp. 64 (top right), 65 (bottom left); NASA, p. 65 (top left); Columbia University, p. 65 (top right); Jean Matheny, p. 66; Mark Olencki, Olencki Graphics, p. 69; South Carolina Land Resources Commission, p. 71.